Daddies, Demons, and The Dawn

ayana walker

BookLeaf
Publishing

India | USA | UK

Daddies, Demons, and The Dawn © 2024
ayana walker

All rights reserved.

No part of this publication may be
reproduced, stored in a retrieval system, or
transmitted, in any form or by any means,
electronic, mechanical, photocopying,
recording or otherwise, without the prior
written permission of the presenters.

ayana walker asserts the moral right to be
identified as author of this work.

Presentation by *BookLeaf Publishing*

Web: www.bookleafpub.com

E-mail: info@bookleafpub.com

ISBN: 9789360945978

First edition 2024

ACKNOWLEDGEMENT

In the pursuit of constructing this collection of verses, I owe immense gratitude to the exceptional individuals who have enriched my poetic journey with their support, inspiration, and resolute encouragement. Their contributions have been essential in forming the soul of these stanzas. To Machelle Brown, Arayna Ford, Eva Turner, Alicia Nicole, Denise Cristobal, G. "Scott", Debbie Nguyen, and Kristina LaGue – thank you for your invaluable presence on this poetic odyssey.

Machelle Brown, your thoughtful reflections have been a guiding light, illuminating the path to expression. Arayna Ford, your artistic spirit has infused this collection with a unique vibration. Eva Turner, your boundless creativity has been a wellspring of inspiration, shaping the contours of these lines. Alicia Nicole, your steadfast belief in the power of words has been a constant source of motivation.

Denise Cristobal, your enthusiasm, encouragement, and feedback have literally meant the world to me. G. "Scott", your unique perspective and creative exchanges have added a layer of richness to this collection. Your friendship and artistic collaboration have been a true blessing. Debbie Nguyen, your support has been a pillar of strength throughout this creative endeavor. Your belief in my abilities has been a driving force.

Kristina LaGue, who would have thought that twenty-five years after our paths crossed, I would be able to tap into the youthful exuberance of my 8-year-old self? This process would not have started without our re-connection and the tiny spark you nurtured in me.

Together, you form a constellation of champions, and I am deeply thankful for the energy you have invested in this poetic endeavor.

With unyielding appreciation,
ayana walker

the healer

oh, i'm a harmony
of dark and twisted reveries
holding my inner child's hand
visiting rooms to show
her things she has no
business to know
and explaining them
to her gently
in a way a child
can understand

Grounding

Acid
Blunt force trauma
Choking
Drug overdose
Electrocution
Falling
Gunshot wound
Hypothermia
Infection
Journalism
Kraken
Laughter
Myocardial infarction
Naivete
Obfuscation
Pulmonary hemorrhage
Respiratory failure
Suicide
Train wreck
Ulcer
Voodoo
Waves
Xenon
Yobs
Zealot

The Time Before Land

Before time
Before Earth
Before the sun
He was there
An abstract
An idea
Floating through the darkness
A nebulous, formless entity
The universe, the world
Took shape before His eyes
Flora, fauna, and humanity
All linked like chains
God, the father, looked at the matter
That materialized
Pleased with Himself
And sighed with relief
That everything was good

After creation
After the fall
After Cain and Abel
He grew exasperated
"None of these people
Show me the appropriate
Amount of reverence…

Of respect…
They are disobedient
Compelled by their flesh
They don't remember
The vast, silent
Seemingly unending blackness
From which we emerged."
Like a small child
Grown frustrated with their toys
He opened up the heavens
And let the clouds weep
On the planet
To wipe out all of the errors
A new, fresh start

If our heavenly father
Is so quick to
Commit wanton genocide,
Does He deserve our worship?

Saboteur

Sowing the seeds
Of my own fulfillment
And overwatering the ground
To stamp out my joy
If the fruit never appears
I've spared myself from
The disappointment of
Taking care of something
Properly
And waiting
To see the results

Rewind

He said, "Not at all. I did what I did. No shame here. Please stop contacting me. I want nothing from you. Not now. Not ever. Enjoy your life. I will not be in it. Peace to you. You are emotional. Like women are. No logic or sound reason."

No, no, no… Before that

Dropping off food
And a care package
Housewarming gifts
When I'm running
On empty
Noticing how frail
You feel
When I give
You a hug
Hoping this small
Token of humanity
Is enough
To keep you
Tethered to
This reality

Go further back…

You coming over
To spend the night
With your girlfriend
The one I really like
The one that is good for you
"We're a packaged deal," you say
Make sure my housemate
Doesn't try anything
My housemate
All 140 pounds of him
Soaking wet
Notices the male
Presence in the home
We share
I am grateful
For masculinity
When it is
Not ego driven
When it is
Not corrupted
When you leave
Later the next day
I wear
A necklace with a blade
While I'm washing dishes
Or walking to the bathroom
Preparing a meal

Sweeping the hardwood floors

Backtrack a bit. What came before?

You text me
That there's a lot
On your mind these days
How you can't stay
Where you live right now
"It's too complicated."
You come stay with me
Fill my little apartment
With all your fire
Tiny ember
All your warmth
Making delicious
Pots of zuppa toscana
And encouraging me
To have my fill
Eagerly watching
As I take that
First slurp of soup
It dances on my palate
I smile
From kitchen to dining room
A big, toothy grin
So do you
"I feel safe here.
Secure. Stable.

Thanks for letting me
Get myself together
On your couch, sis."

Before then?

The Fillmore house
I'd been in SF
For about a year
Remember how
Isolated I felt
When I got here
18 with a suitcase
And a cheap futon
I didn't want you
To have to feel
That creeping loneliness
Didn't want the tar
Of our hometown
To trap you there
To smother you
To keep you small
You go back home
And visit mom
One weekend
Before the 1st of the month
That visit serves
As your tacit
30 day notice

I work
Until the sweat pools
On my brow
Labor myself directly
Into a hospital bed
Walking pneumonia
They tell me
I need to rest
But my rent has
Recently doubled
A byproduct
Of your visit home
I double down and double over
End up in the ER
Twice more
In a span of
About 3 months
The bills don't care
If you're falling apart
They come fast and furious
Delighted at each
Time they can
Make me stay up
For 48 hours straight
Work, school, work, work, school

What precedes that?

You and I

Living on Lexington
Going to separate high schools
Yours is less than 10 minutes
From our home
Mine is about 45 minutes
Away on my feet
For some reason
You are late
To class
More frequently
Than you're on time
I wake you up
In the mornings
Before I walk
Our sister to the bus stop
When I get back home
Sometimes you've fallen
Back to sleep
I wake you up
Once more
Gently, in a sing-songy voice
Some days the veil
Between realms is so thin
That you jump up
Upon entering this
Side of consciousness
With your fists clenched
Throwing savage punches
In my direction

You never connect
But I get more
Weary every time
It happens
I wonder what
You're fighting in your dreams

Go back further

We live
Across the street
From the cemetery
It's quiet, mostly
You and I rise early
Have our football gear
Already packed
Put together our backpacks
And make that trek
To the other side of town
We chat about our classes
And our friends
We fill the time after school
With whatever we want
Before it is time to go to practice
We're on different teams
Because I'm a year older
People ask you if you're my brother…
Ain't you Ayana's bro?
You've always been your own person

Previously

You scream at the
Top of your lungs
Every morning
As mom drops me off
At preschool
Cry, kick, howl
Such big feelings
For a 3 year old
After a couple weeks
Of this daily disaster
Ms. Jodi makes an offer for
You to join my preschool class
The hollering stops
And you join me
On that little circular mat
We sing songs
You learn your letters and numbers
You hold my hand
Hug me
We are inseparable
We are damn near
The same person
We are that close
That connected
That interdependent
On several weekend afternoons

We wake together
After naps
And morning activities
You, my brilliant, athletic brother
Somersault yourself out of your crib
A sneaking smile across your face
We push that heavy
Chair to the front door
You climb up it
Unlock the egress
Crack the portal
To the outside world
Maneuver ourselves
Around the chair, through the entrance
We run
Laughing, giggling
Past the grassy opening
Behind the apartment
We grow tired
And we keep exploring
Make it to the bench
Near the basketball tree
We climb onto the bench
You rest your head
On my shoulder
Mom finds us minutes later
In that exact pose

Do you remember when we were stars, little brother?

Siren

At the deepest depths with you,
I am defenseless
Disgusted by all of my wet clay emotions
The tides under the spell of your moonlight
Energetically porous, letting things permeate me
And go through me that wouldn't
Have had access previously

My fears
While not entirely real, somewhat imagined…
That I'm carrying more than you are
That I'm more invested
That there's something in the
Back of my head that is
Worried about being disposable
To the people I love
Being a single use friend,discard after use
That I'll get tossed without
Consideration or appreciation
And you will continue on with your life
While I fall apart completely

Catch and Release

I want to sit on your couch
Us facing each other
You sitting on my lap
With your hands on my scalp
While I give you kisses
On every inch of you
I can see

I want you to touch me
Like I am an oasis
And you've been traversing the desert
For days on end
Greedily, frantically, with no concern
For where your fingertips
Connect with my flesh

I want you to smell me
My sweet, earthy fullness
Rising to your nostrils
Inhale me, drink me in
Like my scent is
The only thing separating
You from your own demise

I want you to taste me
Bittersweet with hints of sodium
From tears or sweat
It does not matter
Ingest me
So there is always
A part of me inside you

I want you to hear me
A symphony of sighs
Breathing coming in gulps
Sound waves
Crashing and collapsing into
Desperate carnal hymns
Chants that cannot be repeated

I want you to see me
Flushed, ripe, and radiant
Glowing from within
A silhouette of pure light
Magnetic energy pulsing
Flickering and somehow
Never losing intensity

One Above All

Black is when you see the sky
It is depression and a sigh
The color of someone's skin
Lets us see hurt or sin
A blackbird so delicate and light
Will see the stars in the air tonight
Black is how we feel or see
Black can be our destiny
Black is sorrow in your heart
Black is kind and forever smart
Black is when we see the sky
A gentle kiss
A wave goodbye

The Last Supper

Twelve folks gather
Around me
Around the table
None of whom are disciples
Three wise men
Four mystics
And five marauders
They are dressed
In robes and sandals
I wear no clothes
But my hair is hidden
Under purple stained linen
It is a celebration
"One of ya'll is going
To betray me
For petty cash."
I announce to the group
As we all take our seats

I watch
While the tension
Creeps in like fog
Eyes flit about
As if to say
Is it me?
Is it them?
Who can it be?

I pick up my
Knife from the table
And arduously start to cut
A sliver of flesh
From shoulder cap
To elbow
Meticulously divide it
Into thirteen pieces
I ask everyone seated
To take a piece and
Pass it around
One would think
This ragtag bunch
Of miscreants were
All vegan
With the way they
Hesitantly examine my meat
This is my body
Which I've broken for you
Eat this
The dinner party
Is nothing if not
Obedient
We chew, chew, chew
And swallow
The unease in
The air is still palpable
I have collected

Blood from my wound
In my cup
I take a sip
Pass the chalice to my right
Instruct the crew
To lift me to their lips
And drink

This shared ritual
Has done nothing
To assuage the
Lingering doubt
And relative paranoia
I can feel
The thoughts
Running through
Everyone's brains
Yes, I know who
Will sell me out
At a discounted rate
Yes, my father
Is aware of what He
Is putting me through
But I am
Going off script
I can't trust Him
He raped my underage
Mother to create me
Yes, Joseph will never

Recover if my fate comes
So we are all going
To sit here until
The traitor makes
A confession
Backstabbers are
Not generally
Known for their bravery

"Let's cut to the chase,
It's you, Judas"
I exclaim after
Waiting for over
An hour
I am drunk
On my own
Blood and wine
I know how
This particular story
Is supposed to end
I ask two of the wise men
To string the turncoat
Up on a tree
So we can hang him
And I can go to sleep
I have a big day
Ahead of me
They oblige me
And that snake

With ropes
Around his throat
Meets his end
In the same manner
But earlier in the timeline
Than planned

Listen up
There is a rip
In the time-space continuum
My Father cannot interfere
We are all getting
Out of here
Alive
The only thing
You need is
The faith
Of a mustard seed
To follow me
Into the darkness
Where we all came from
Many millennia ago
Me and
The eleven remaining guests
Link hands
Cross the threshold
We emerge
On the other side
As pure energy

17

Capitalism's
Phallus gets sucked and I think
Are we all free yet?

Looking Glass

My breath
Ragged and uneven
Air flowing through my nostrils
Onto the nape of your neck
The walls have ears
But do they have mouths?
If I closed all the doors,
Could I get the walls to speak volumes about us?

Permutations

If I wake up
And the pen whispers to me
That today she is a guillotine
The only offerings she
Will accept are ligaments,
Body parts, and hot, thick blood
Who am I
As her faithful servant
To deny her the worship
She so righteously deserves?

If I go to sleep
And the pen screams to me
That today he is a lullaby
He requires an ABAB rhyme scheme
Syllables as soft as a butterfly
Don't question if it is all just a dream
Close your precious eyes, hush a bye
Let the ink slowly build your self esteem
Light up your mind like the 4th of July
Everything is never what it seems

If I go for a jog
And the pen proclaims to me
That today they are my running shoes
The only job they have
Is to make sure I get
Wherever I'm going
In one piece, supported
Preferably looking pretty fresh
Can I be sure to clean
Them after each run through the muck?

If I sit down for a meal
And the pen mumbles to me
That today she is apathy
She can't be bothered with
The emotional rollercoaster of it all
Of making something from nothing
The pressure is too much
It is easier to be impervious
To everything outside of her control
Numb tastes like a gourmet feast

If I flip a coin
And the pen chuckles to me
That today he is destiny
He is three crones holding
The thread of fate in his hands
I can't make heads or tails of it

I release myself from the
Expectation of being a fortune teller
My crystal ball forever clouded
We write the futures we want to see

Eve

I have this recurring dream
That I see
My twice zombie father
Walking down the street
I approach him casually
Pull my blade
From my pocket
Slit his throat
And bathe in his blood
A baptism of sorts

I wonder
If he would have
Stuck around
Would I have all
Of these delightful, violent fantasies?
Maybe that is why he
Could never be
Anything resembling
A father to me
The poisoned apple does not
Fall too far from the tree

Arinna Ra

As a matter of fact
If you're going to eye
Fuck me that hard
I should charge
A motherfucking cover
You wet blanket ass broad

Hard to tell
Who is colder or harder
When you're in the
Vicinity of a soaring saucer
Bossy, saucy, and glossy
But never pressed
Negative stress
Sitting powerfully and purposefully
In lotus flower blossom
Absolute zero degree zen assertion
My little Waka Flocka flame

Look there!
It's a bird!
It's a plane!
No, look here

She's a fallen star
And she's fallen so far
Now all she wants is
A place to call home in Rome
A place to free her mind on her own time
And a Polly Pocket dream house

Because I'm a phenom at 5'2"
With a seven footer's attitude
I get what I want
I like what I see
And if you really like me
I strongly suggest
With a "S" on my chest
That you, mighty sun
Invest in glasses
To see me through

Excavation

You don't be ripping off clothes
To be all soft, slow, and sensual
I do. Can. Enjoy from time to time
Also enjoy the urgency,
Primacy of my heart pounding
Out of my chest and someone
Matching the tempo

Fistfuls of hair
And less words exchanged than
A mime's performance
Silent like the grave
Outer space
Devoid of language altogether
Almost anonymous

I don't want to recognize
Myself after the fact
Sweat dripping down my spine
You dripping at the same time
{Just trying to ride out this wave of
Morning arousal in a creative way}
On your face
Or perhaps beneath you

Your fingertips exploring
Corners of my corporeality
Some paths paved
Others feral
New lands to be
Discovered and conquered

Or lands where the soil
Needs tilling
Needs hoeing
Needs water
And sunshine
Nitrogen

My fixed, sinewy beginnings
Moving, stirring
Under the watchful eye
Of a skilled arborist
I imagine
When a tree cums
It looks like breathing
The ground opening up
And then contracting once more
Roots shifting and
Repositioning themselves
Leaves drifting to the earth

Marvel

Fe-male?
No, I'm Iron Man
Harder than adamantium
Playboy philanthropist
Watching the Libra full moon
Grinning lycanthropist

You wanna run with the feral dogs?
You think you can keep pace in my pack?
Keep dreaming, calvin and hobbes
Sprinters with stamina and we are all black
It's not on me, it's in me-vibranium
Let me introduce the team to the stadium…

My wife, MLB, plays for the major league
That's Rogue, make sure she keeps her fingers
covered
Power over death in the palm of her hands,
doublespeak
She'll take your life at my request and sleep
unencumbered
I feel invincible with her in my pocket
My heart on my sleeve, tucked like a locket

Pops? He's Magneto- always ready for a war
Believes in the delusion of his own supremacy
I know he's smiling up at me from hell, that boar
My mother, Loki, being gracious with her
clemency
Goddess of mischief, my hands down top tier
trickster
She's more a god of stories these days since fate
betwixt her

My sister has her eyes on other planets, Captain
Marvel
She's small and mighty; lighting up the sky
every night
Her husband's the Black Panther, crown jewel of
Wakanda
The heart shaped herb keeps him on the side of
what is right
Their progeny? My nephew, that's Prodigy
The most wild by way of camaraderie

Big bro is lean, smokes green, an Incredible
Hulk
Beware his temper- you won't like him when
he's mad
Flattens the city, then goes to the corner to sulk
Lil' bro's the Silver Surfer, an alien, aren't you
glad?
All that cosmic power, dude is in his own reality

While he's scouting worlds, please remind him
of his humanity

There's the crew, the squad,the team, the gang
We're not the Avengers, not the Defenders
We come through and manage the chaos. You
rang?
Only champions here; there are no contenders
All the wolves fall in line, know their place in
my pack
The elders know all the best leaders lead from
the back

Frogs

But I am me
A multi-hyphenate
More than a triple threat
Brain like an Ivy
Body like an
Out of work
Video vixen

You always
Upset at the attention
I garner
Shuffling through your insecurities
Like Pokemon cards
Angry at the
Erections around me
Unsettled
At the women
In leather
Flirting with me

Newsflash!
I am fine as frog hair
There will always be
Hard and wet things
Surrounding me

You said you would not
Be at peace until
I was resting peacefully

How dare you?
You have some damn nerve
To threaten me!
The wretched gall
And unmitigated audacity

You will NEVER know peace
That is a promise
A curse
A fucking guarantee

You are FOREVER
In debt to me
To my talents
My aura
My exquisite energy

Remember that
You gorgeous, vile tree
Ground is weak to water
You'll always be weak to me
Beloved
Red, brown mahogany

Weight

How do you
Carry all that weight?
With panache
And grace
And a gun in your face

She murdered all the
Weaker iterations of herself
Downloaded their memories
Buried them
A graveyard of her
Less evolved selves
Planted trees nearby
From time to time
She digs her selves back up
Positions her alters
To sit and chat
When it's all said and done
She places herself into
That makeshift grave
A pauper's resting place
And she shovels
The earth back onto herself

Strong hands

Pull her up those six feet
Dust her off completely
And sit her up next to
An adjacent tombstone
"I don't understand why headquarters
Continues to give me these bogus assignments."
She overhears
As her alter
Gives her a once over
She is unable to speak
Unable to signal to her
Alter that she is still alive
At least she thinks she is
In this peculiar between
Realms existence she finds
Herself in
Mud covers her limbs
Then her abdomen
And finally her face

How do you
Carry all that weight?
With panache
And grace
And a gun in your face

She is sharply dressed
For a woman that just dug
Up a corpse and buried it again

Shiny, leather boots and
A water-repellent trench coat
A sleek, large bag
Packed with some supplies
And a couple of
Just in case passports
She gathers herself
Closes her eyes
For a brief moment
Walks to her car
And then makes
That miserable commute
To the casino
It's the last
Box to check on
Her to-do list
She parks
Saunters up to the
Designated roulette table
And places one chip on red
She has left the felt
Before the dealer
Declares she is a winner

The next morning
She wakes up
Bright and early
Does some halfhearted stretches
She's excited

Today, she gets to
Use a real weapon
And the best part
No digging
Strictly shoot and bag
She brushes her hair
Daydreaming about doing
A good job
And getting that
Promotion everyone
Has been chatting about
She leaves the flat
Disappears like a ghost
She starts to stalk
The latest mark

How do you
Carry all that weight?
With panache
And grace
And a gun in your face

This mark is
So nondescript
She imagines the target
Must have fallen in with
A bad crowd
To end up on her radar
In her crosshairs

A job is a job
The countryside is quiet
Not many people this
Far outside the city
The earth is
Still moist from
Yesterday's downpour
The mark pulls over
Near a well manicured
Meadow of lush foliage
She pulls over as well
Some ninety feet behind
Her intended target
She focuses
Squeezes the trigger
And fixates as the bullet
Barrels through the mark's brain
For a split second
She sees herself
With a hot lead hole
Ripping through her 3rd eye

She blinks
Blinks again
Her eyes are not working
There is only blackness
An abyss, a dark void
There are sounds though
Underwater noises, voices

Coming from somewhere external
A glimmer of brightness
Expanding quickly
Enveloping her
And then pressure
A sudden whooshing feeling
Fluorescent lights blind her
As she cries out
With all the strength
Her lungs can muster
"A healthy baby girl!"
She looks at her tiny fingers
They are unrecognizable
As is she
She wails out
Like a banshee
Signaling a fresh death

Dog Pound

This is not my sister
It's me
You and I don't share blood
Never have, never will
You're cut from a different
Cloth that is obsolete
Like you
A relic
A has been
A nobody
Because that is all
You ever were and
All you'll ever be

The fact that you're telling your seed
Anything about this just shows
How much of a little punk you are
And you can't even get the
Message right because you don't
Read too well
That's never been your
Area of expertise

Words of advice to your
Country bumpkin, wannabe gangster self:

Keep your bitches on a short leash
Just now, calls to animal control
Are being intercepted by vigilantes
Don't make me pick your bitches up
Off the street in my van
And ransom them back to you
Find your backbone
To make sure your bitches don't
Attack each other
The women around you
Are weak
They will allow you to move in
The way you have because they
Are irreparably broken
So are you
You are pathetic
Pitiful
A fucking pansy
I will run you out of this town
Or out of your mind
Whichever is easiest on my pen
You are cursed
Damned
Doomed
Run and tell that
You rat

My Scent Lingers

I asked her to
Tell me what I
Smell like to her

Salt from the ocean
Exhaust fumes
Iron
Sweat
Day old dreams
Whimsy
Campfires
Coconut milk
Quantum physics on vinyl
Men's deodorant
Dopamine

No longer like
Waffle cones,
Youthful exuberance,
And simpler times
You will always feel
Like home to me
I know traces of you
Will be found in my marrow

Transmutation

It was a flash
An illusion
For a split second
You took the form
Of a demon
I've been unable to tame
And I thought
I'm not _____ enough to
Handle this
Lying there
Nude
I folded into myself
Like origami
I turned myself
Into a crane
What business
Does a demon have
With this fragile, papery
Bird-wings outstretched
Toward the sky?
I flapped
Picking up momentum
My eyes on the sun
Tears falling over themselves
The glamour divorced

Itself from you
Leaving you in a form
I'm more familiar with
The infinite sky
Hugging a flying fowl